DECK
ESSENTIALS

BLACK & DECKER®

QUICK STEPS™

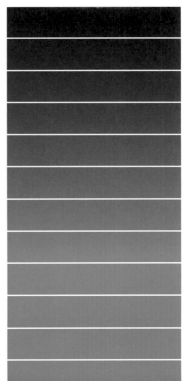

COWLES
Creative Publishing
A Division of Cowles Enthusiast Media, Inc.

Credits

Copyright © 1997
Cowles Creative Publishing, Inc.
Formerly Cy DeCosse Incorporated
5900 Green Oak Drive
Minnetonka, Minnesota 55343
1-800-328-3895
All rights reserved
Printed in U.S.A.

COWLES
Creative Publishing
A Division of Cowles Enthusiast Media, Inc.

President/COO: Nino Tarantino
Executive V.P./Editor-in-Chief: William B. Jones

Created by: The Editors of Cowles Creative Publishing, Inc.,
in cooperation with Black & Decker. is
a trademark of the Black & Decker Corporation and is
used under license.

Printed on American paper by:
 Quebecor Printing
 99 98 97 96 / 5 4 3 2 1

COWLES
Enthusiast Media

President/COO: Philip L. Penny

Books available in this series:

Wiring Essentials
Plumbing Essentials
Carpentry Essentials
Painting Essentials
Flooring Essentials
Landscape Essentials
Masonry Essentials
Door & Window Essentials
Roof & Siding Essentials
Deck Essentials
Porch & Patio Essentials
Built-In Essentials

Contents

Introduction

Deck Basics 4

Decking Patterns 6

Stairways 8

Railings 9

Lumber Basics 10

Pressure-treated Lumber 12

Redwood & Cedar 13

Lumber Size & Deck Planning 14

Hardware & Fasteners 16

Concrete 18

Tool Basics 21

Design & Planning

Creating Site Drawings 22

Drawing Design Plans 25

Building Decks

Installing a Ledger 28

Locating Post Footings 34

Digging & Pouring Footings 40

Setting Posts 44

Installing a Beam 50

Hanging Joists 54

Laying Decking 61

Building Stairs 64

Installing a Deck Railing 70

Lumber & Materials Checklist 78

Index 79

Deck Basics

Building a deck is one of the most popular do-it-yourself projects. With a few carpentry skills and a basic knowledge of tools, any homeowner can construct a durable and beautiful deck.

This book provides valuable information on deck structure, materials used, and planning tips, while complete step-by-step instructions show how to construct each component of a deck. From installing the ledger and laying out footings to putting the final touches on the deck railing, we give you the essential know-how to construct a beautiful and durable deck of your own.

Parts of a Deck

Structural parts of a deck include posts, beams, ledgers, and joists. They support and distribute the weight of the deck. For economy and durability, use pressure-treated lumber for these parts. The other parts of a deck include the decking, facing, railings, and stairway. Use redwood or cedar for these visible parts.

Ledgers anchor an attached deck to a house. Ledgers support one end of all joists.

Concrete footings with post anchors support the weight of the deck and hold the deck posts in place. They are made by pouring concrete into tube forms. Local climates and building codes determine depth of footings. **Post anchors** should be made of galvanized steel to resist corrosion.

Posts transfer the weight of the deck to the footings. They are attached to the post anchors with galvanized nails, and to the beam with lag screws.

Beams provide the main structural support for the deck. A beam is usually made from a pair of 2 × 8s or 2 × 10s attached to the deck posts.

Joists support the decking. For an attached deck, the joists are fastened at one end to the **ledger,** and at the other end to the **header joist**. The **outside joists** can be covered with redwood or cedar **facing** boards for appearance.

Decking is the main feature of any deck. The decking boards are attached to the joists with galvanized screws or nails.

Railing parts include **railing posts** and **balusters** attached to the header and outside joists, a horizontal **rail**, and a **cap**. Building codes may require railings on decks 24" or more above ground level.

A stairway is made from a pair of **stringers** fastened to the side of the deck, and a series of **treads** attached to the stringers with metal cleats.

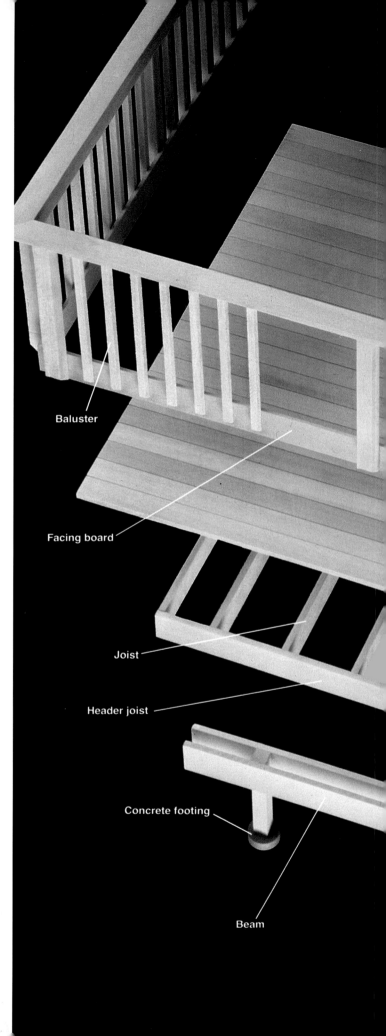

Baluster

Facing board

Joist

Header joist

Concrete footing

Beam

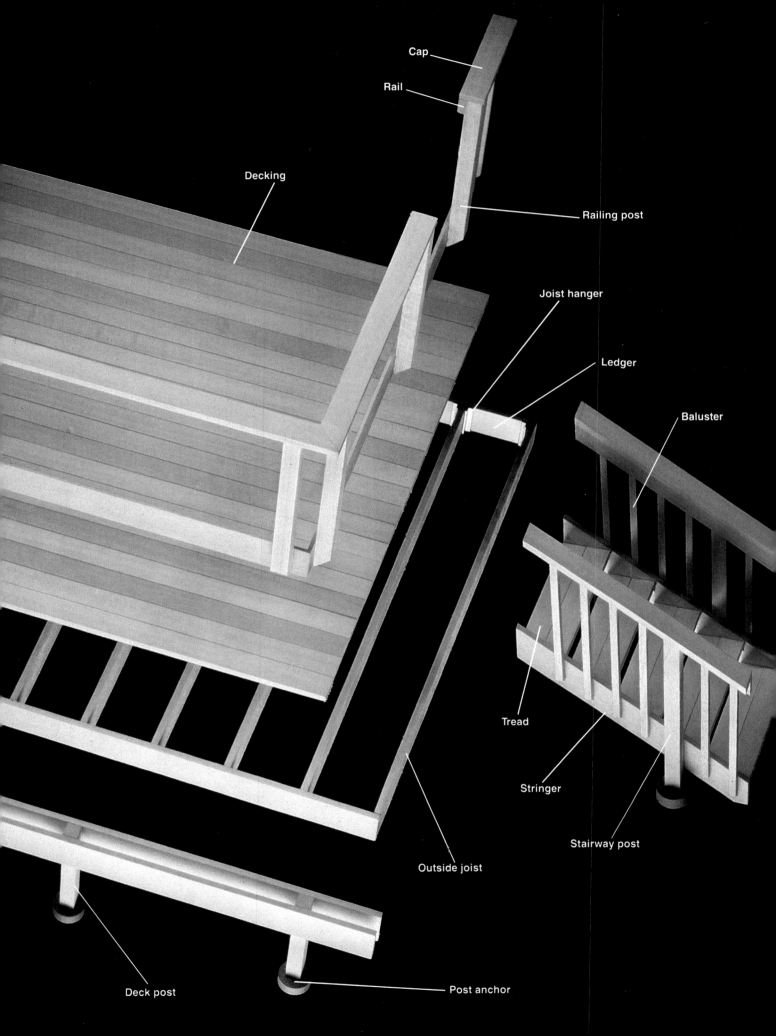

Cap

Rail

Decking

Railing post

Joist hanger

Ledger

Baluster

Tread

Stringer

Outside joist

Stairway post

Deck post

Post anchor

Decking Patterns

Decking is an important element of a deck, and can be installed using a variety of board sizes and design patterns. The decking pattern determines the spacing and layout of the joists. For example, a normal, straight decking pattern requires joists that are spaced 16" on-center. A diagonal decking

Diagonal pattern adds visual interest to a deck. Diagonal patterns require joists that are spaced closer together than for straight patterns.

Double joist

Blocking

Parquet pattern requires double joists and blocking to provide a supporting surface for attaching the butted ends of decking boards.

pattern requires that the joist spacing be 12" on-center. Parquet patterns and some other designs may require extra support, like double joists or extra blocking. For sturdy, flat decking, use 2 × 4 or 2 × 6 lumber. Thinner lumber is more likely to twist or cup.

Framed opening for a tree requires extra blocking between joists. Short joists are attached to blocking with joist hangers.

Border pattern gives an elegant, finished look to a deck. Install trim joists to support the border decking.

Stairways

A stairway provides access to a deck from the yard or patio. Its position also helps establish traffic patterns across the deck.

Build the stairway with lumber that matches the rest of the deck. If possible, stair treads should use the same board pattern as the surface decking. On decks more than 24" high, local codes may require stairway handrails.

Platform steps feature wide treads. Each step is built on a framework of posts and joists.

Stairway Styles

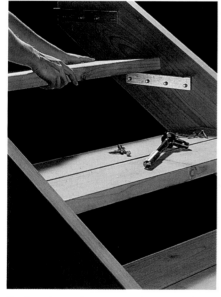

Open steps have metal cleats that hold the treads between the stringers. The treads on this stairway are built with 2 × 6s to match the surface decking.

Boxed steps, built with notched stringers and solid risers, give a finished look to a deck stairway. Predrill ends of treads to prevent splitting.

Long stairways sometimes require landings. A landing is a small platform to which both flights of stairs are attached.

Railings

Railings usually are required by building code on any deck that is more than 24" high. Select a railing design that fits the style of your home.

For example, on a low, ranch-style house, choose a deck railing with wide, horizontal rails. On a Tudor-style home with a steep roof, choose a railing with closely spaced, vertical balusters.

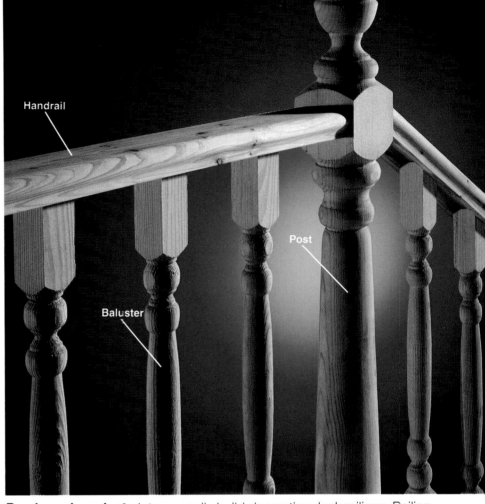

Preshaped products let you easily build decorative deck railings. Railing products include shaped handrails, balusters, and posts.

Railing Styles

Vertical balusters with posts and rails are a good choice for houses with strong vertical lines. A vertical baluster railing like the one shown above is a good choice where children will be present.

Horizontal railings are often used on low, ranch-style homes. Horizontal railing is made of vertical posts, two or more wide horizontal rails, and a railing cap.

Lattice panels add a decorative touch to a deck. They also provide extra privacy.

Lumber Basics

Lumber used to construct a deck must be resistant to rot and insect damage. The three types of wood recommended for deck construction are: heartwood grade redwood, heartwood cedar, and pressure-treated lumber.

The reddish heartwoods of both redwood and cedar have natural decay resistance. The sapwood of redwood and cedar is lighter in color than the heart-wood and has less resistance to decay. Sapwood must be treated with a clear sealer-preservative if used outdoors.

Pressure-treated lumber is treated with chemical preservatives. The preservative most often used for decking lumber is chromated copper arsenate, identified by the label "CCA."

Inspect each piece of lumber, and return any pieces that are severely warped or cracked. Avoid any boards that have large knots, especially where strength is essential, like joists or stairways.

Ingrown knot

Inspect lumber for flaws. Sight along each board to check for warping and twisting. Return any boards with serious flaws. Check for large or loose knots. Boards used for structural parts should be knot-free (clear), or should have only small knots that are tight and ingrown.

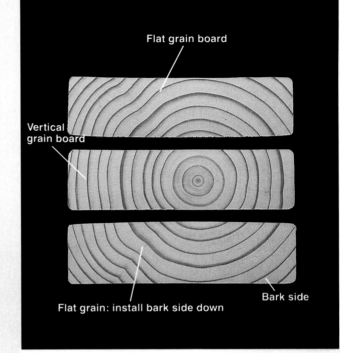

Flat grain board

Vertical grain board

Bark side

Flat grain: install bark side down

Check end grain of decking boards. Boards with flat grain tend to "cup," and can trap standing water if not installed properly. Recent research indicates that flat grain boards cup toward the bark side (not away from it, as was previously thought in the industry), and should be installed so the bark side faces down.

Store lumber so that it stays dry and warp-free. Use supports to keep the wood stack a few inches off the ground. Use spacer blocks to support each row of lumber, and to allow air circulation between boards. Cover the lumber stack with heavy plastic or a water-proof tarp.

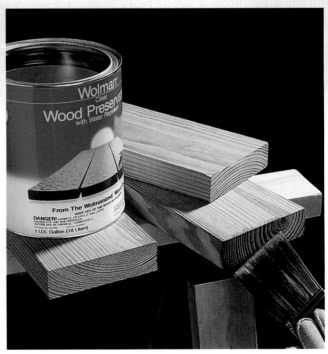

Seal cut edges of all lumber, including pressure-treated wood, by brushing on clear liquid sealer-preservative. Chemicals used in pressure treatment do not always penetrate completely. Sealer-preservative protects all types of wood from rot.

Pressure-treated Lumber

Pressure-treated lumber is the strongest and least expensive choice for deck lumber. Pressure-treated lumber resists rot and insects and is an excellent building material for outdoor use.

Treated lumber is created by forcing chemical preservatives into it under high pressure. The most common treatment uses chromated copper arsenate, identified by the label "CCA." The preservative usually gives the wood a green color, which fades with time. Or, you can stain pressure-treated wood in a variety of colors.

Pressure-treated lumber is rated by the amount of chemical retained by the wood. For decks, choose lumber with a retention level of .40, approved for direct ground contact. This is sometimes signified by the code "LP 22" stamped on the wood.

Pressure-treated lumber can be used to build the entire deck; or, it can be used only for posts, beams, and joists, with redwood or cedar used for decking, stairways, facing, and railings.

Caution:
The chemicals in pressure-treated lumber are toxic. Wear eye protection, a particle mask, and long sleeves and pants to avoid contact with sawdust from pressure-treated wood.

Grade stamp for pressure-treated lumber lists the type of preservative used and the chemical retention level of the wood. Look for "CCA" label indicating that chromated copper arsenate is the preservative. Make sure lumber carries the label "LP 22," or ".40 retention." Other information found on grade stamp includes proper exposure rating, and name and location of treating company.

Redwood

Redwood is an attractive wood often used for outdoor structures. The heartwood has a brownish red color and is naturally resistant to decay. The cream-colored sapwood should be treated with wood preservative when used in a deck.

Quality redwood is somewhat expensive, so it is often used only for visible parts of the deck, like decking and railings.

Redwood is available in more than 30 grades. "Construction heart" or "merchantable heart" are medium-quality grades that are good choices for a deck.

Cedar

The cedar species recommended for decks include red cedar and incense cedar. Cedar has a light brown appearance, with an attractive grain. Because it ages to a uniform silver-gray, cedar is often used where a weathered appearance is desired.

Heartwood cedar is naturally resistant to decay. Sapwood cedar is white or cream-colored, and should be treated with wood preservative when used in a deck.

Cedar can be used for the visible surfaces of the deck. For structural members like joists, beams, and posts, use pressure-treated lumber.

Grade stamp for redwood lists wood dryness, lumber grade, and membership association. Redwood should be certified "KILN DRIED" or "DRY"; and graded as clear redwood (CLR RWD), construction heartwood (CONST HT), merchantable heartwood (MERCH HT), or construction redwood (CONST RWD).

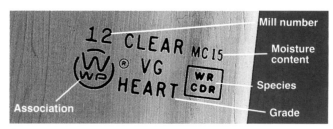

Grade stamp for cedar lists the lumber mill number, the moisture content, the species, the lumber grade, and membership association. Western red cedar (WRC) or incense cedar (INC) used in decks should be graded as heartwood (HEART) with a maximum moisture content of 15% (MC 15).

Lumber Size & Deck Planning

A deck has seven major structural parts: the **ledger, decking, joists,** one or more **beams, posts, stairway stringers,** and **stairway treads.** To create a working design plan, you must know the span limits of each part of the deck. The ledger is attached directly to the house and does not have a span limit.

A span limit is the safe distance a board can cross without support from underneath. The maximum safe span depends on the size of the board. For example, 2 × 6 joists spaced 16" on-center can safely span 9' 9", while 2 × 10 joists can span 16' 5".

Begin planning by first choosing size and pattern of the decking. Then determine the size and layout of the joists, beams, and posts, using the span tables on the opposite page. In general, a deck designed with larger-size lumber, like 2 × 12 joists and beams, requires fewer pieces, because the boards have a large span limit.

Nominal	Actual
1 × 4	¾" × 3¾"
1 × 6	¾" × 5¾"
2 × 4	1½" × 3½"
2 × 6	1½" × 5½"
2 × 8	1½" × 7¼"
2 × 10	1½" × 9¼"
2 × 12	1½" × 11¼"
4 × 4	3½" × 3½"
6 × 6	5½" × 5½"

Nominal vs. Actual Lumber Dimensions: When planning a deck, remember that the actual size of lumber is smaller than the nominal size by which lumber is sold. Use the actual dimension when drawing a deck design plan, and use the Lumber & Materials Checklist on page 78 when ordering materials.

Span Limit Tables for Deck Lumber

Recommended Decking Span Between Joists:
Decking boards can be made from a variety of lumber sizes. For a basic deck use 2 × 4 or 2 × 6 lumber with joists spaced 16" apart.

Decking Boards	Recommended Span
1 × 4 or 1 × 6, laid straight	16"
1 × 4 or 1 × 6, laid diagonal	12"
2 × 4 or 2 × 6, laid straight	16"
2 × 4 or 2 × 6, laid diagonal	12"
2 × 4, laid on edge	24"

Maximum Joist Span Between Supports: Maximum joist span between supports depends on the size of the joists and the spacing between joists. For example, a deck with 2 × 8 joists spaced 16" apart requires supports no more than 12' 10" apart. On a cantilevered deck, the joists may extend past the beam by a distance equal to one-third the total length of the joists.

Joist Size	Joist Spacing (on center) 12"	16"	24"
2 × 6	11' 7"	9' 9"	7' 11"
2 × 8	15' 0"	12' 10"	10' 6"
2 × 10	19' 6"	16' 5"	13' 4"

Maximum Beam Span Between Posts: Maximum beam span depends on the size of the beams and their spacing. For example, a deck with a 4 × 8 beam, and joists that span 12 feet should have posts that are no more than 7 feet apart.

Beam Size	Joist Span 6 ft.	8 ft.	10 ft.	12 ft.
4 × 6 (two 2 × 6s)	8 ft.	7 ft.	6 ft.	5 ft.
4 × 8 (two 2 × 8s)	10 ft.	9 ft.	8 ft.	7 ft.
4 × 10 (two 2 × 10s)	12 ft.	11 ft.	10 ft.	9 ft.
4 × 12 (two 2 × 12s)	14 ft.	13 ft.	12 ft.	11 ft.

Recommended Post Size: Choose post size by finding the load area for the deck. To find the load area, multiply the distance between beams by the distance between posts. For example, on a deck that has one beam spaced 10 feet from the ledger, with posts spaced 7 feet apart, the load area is 70. If this deck is less than 6 feet high, the recommended post size is 4 × 4.

Deck Height	Load Area 48	72	96	120	144
Up to 6 ft.	4 × 4	4 × 4	6 × 6	6 × 6	6 × 6
More than 6 ft.	6 × 6	6 × 6	6 × 6	6 × 6	6 × 6

Minimum Stair Stringer Sizes: Size of stair stringers depends on the span of the stairway. For example, if the bottom of the stairway lies 7 feet from the deck, build the stringers from 2 × 12s.

Span of Stairway	Stringer Size
Up to 6 ft.	2 × 10
More than 6 ft.	2 × 12

Recommended Railing Sizes: Size of posts, rails, and caps depends on the spacing of the railing posts. For example, if railing posts are spaced 6 feet apart, use 4 × 4 posts and 2 × 6 rails and caps.

Space Between Railing Posts	Post Size	Cap Size	Rail Size
2 ft. to 3 ft.	2 × 4	2 × 4	2 × 4
3 ft. to 4 ft.	4 × 4	2 × 4	2 × 4
4 ft. to 6 ft.	4 × 4	2 × 6	2 × 6

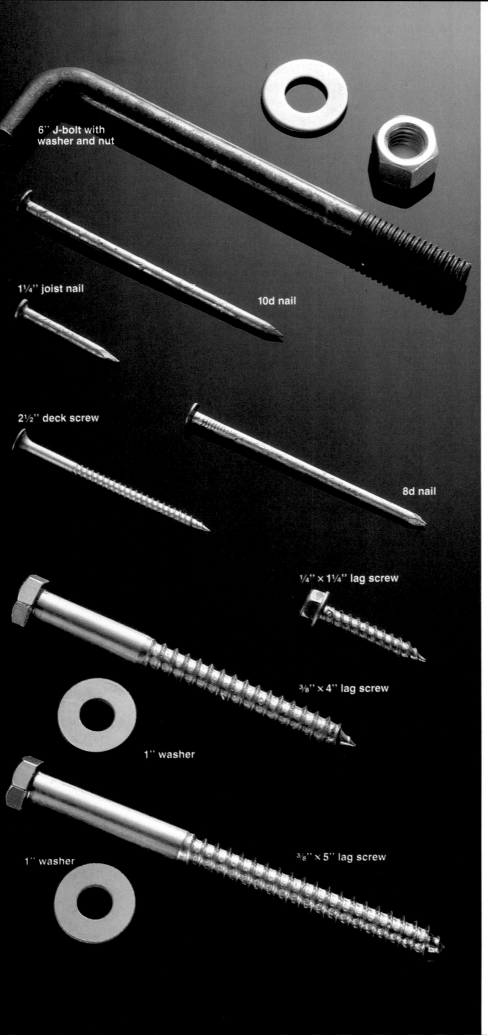

6" J-bolt with washer and nut

1¼" joist nail

10d nail

2½" deck screw

8d nail

¼" × 1¼" lag screw

⅜" × 4" lag screw

1" washer

1" washer

⅜" × 5" lag screw

Hardware & Fasteners

Build your deck with galvanized lumber connectors, nails, and screws. Galvanized metal products resist rust and will not stain the wood.

Metal lumber connectors are used to create strong joints with wood framing members. Post anchors, joist hangers, and brackets are available at lumberyards and home improvement centers. To simplify ordering materials, use the Lumber & Materials Checklist on page 78 to list the items you'll need.

Seal heads of counterbored screws with silicone caulk to prevent water damage.

Hot-dipped galvanized nails (above) have a thick zinc coating and rough surface. Hot-dipped nails will not rust or stain wood.

Deck fasteners (left), include 6" J-bolt with nut and washer, 8d and 10d galvanized nails, 1¼" galvanized joist nail, 2½" corrosion-resistant deck screw, ¼" × 1¼" lag screw, ⅜" × 4" lag screw, ⅜" × 5" lag screw, and 1" washer.

Flashing fits over ledger to protect wood from moisture damage. Top edge of flashing tucks up under the siding.

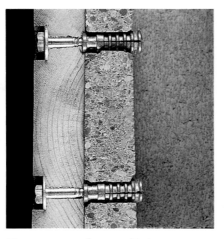

Masonry anchors with lag screws hold the ledger to stone, brick, or concrete blocks.

J-bolts with nuts and washers hold the post anchors to the concrete footings.

Post anchors hold deck posts in place, and raise the base of the posts to help prevent water from entering end grain of wood.

Angle brackets help reinforce header and outside joists. Angle brackets are also used to attach stair stringers to the deck.

Joist hangers are used to attach joists to the ledger and header joist. Double hanger is used when decking pattern requires a double-width joist.

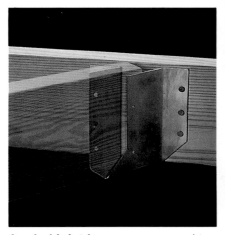

Angled joist hangers are used to frame decks that have unusual angles or decking patterns.

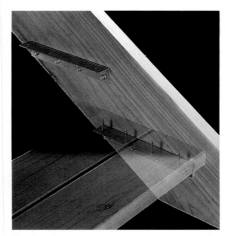

Stair cleats support the treads of deck steps. Cleats are attached to stair stringers with ¼" × 1¼" galvanized lag screws.

Silicone caulk seals lag screw heads and any cracks that may trap water. Choose an exterior-grade caulk rated for lifetime use.

Concrete

Use concrete to make solid footings that will support the weight of the deck. Concrete for footings is made from a mixture of portland cement, sand, and coarse gravel (¼" to 1½" in diameter). These materials can be purchased separately and mixed at home, or you can buy bags containing the premixed dry ingredients. For larger amounts, buy ready-mixed concrete in trailer loads.

For most deck projects, mixing you own concrete is easy and inexpensive. Mix concrete in a wheelbarrow or with a power mixer, available at tool rental centers.

The estimation charts on the opposite page give approximate volumes of concrete. You may have a small amount of concrete left over after pouring post footings. Use the Lumber & Materials Checklist on page 78 when purchasing materials.

Mix concrete ingredients in a wheelbarrow. Use a ratio of 1 part portland cement (A), 2 parts sand (B), and 3 parts coarse gravel (C). Or, use the cubic-foot volumes shown in the chart (page opposite).

Amount of Concrete Needed (cubic feet)

Number of 8" Diameter Footings	Depth of Footings (feet)			
	1	2	3	4
2	¾	1½	2¼	3
3	1	2¼	3½	4½
4	1½	3	4½	6
5	2	3¾	5¾	7½

Concrete Ingredient Amounts

Amount of Concrete Needed (cubic feet)	Dry Ingredients for Self-mix			60-lb. bags of premixed dry concrete
	94-lb. bags of portland cement	Cubic feet of sand	Cubic feet of gravel	
1	⅙	⅓	½	2
2	⅓	⅔	1	4
3	½	1½	3	6
4	¾	1¾	3½	8
5	1	2¼	4½	10
10	2	4½	9	20

Buying & Mixing Concrete

Buy premixed bags of dry concrete for small jobs. A 60-lb. bag creates about ½ of a cubic foot of concrete. A 90-lb. bag creates about ⅔ of a cubic foot.

Rent a power cement mixer to blend large amounts of cement, gravel, sand, and water quickly.

Ratchet wrench & socket

Shovel

Trowel

Metal snips

22-oz. claw hammer

32-oz. masonry hammer

Cat's paw

Hoe

16-ft. tape measure

50-ft. tape measure

Caulk gun

Rubber mallet

Clamshell posthole digger

Combination square

Mason's string

Compass

Plumb bob

Flat pry bar

Line level

Scratch awl

Torpedo level

Putty knife

Chalk line

1"chisel

Level

Framing square

Hand tools for deck building should have heavy-duty construction. Metal tools should be made from high-carbon steel with smoothly finished surfaces. Buy quality hand tools that are well balanced, and that have tight, comfortably molded handles. There is no substitute for quality.

Tool Basics

With a set of basic hand and power tools, you can complete any of the deck projects shown in this book. You may already own many of the tools needed. If you buy new tools, invest in quality, heavy-duty products that will provide long service.

Some specialty tools, like power miter boxes or reciprocating saws, are available at tool rental centers. Or, they can be purchased at home improvement stores.

Always wear eye protection when using tools. Always wear a particle mask and work gloves when sawing or handling pressure-treated lumber, because the chemicals in the wood are toxic.

Tools for finishing and maintaining a deck include: rubber gloves (A), shop vacuum (B), 14-gauge extension cord (C), pressure sprayer (D), hydraulic jack and handle (E), eye protection (F), scrub brush (G), paint brush (H), particle mask (I), and orbital sander (J).

Power tools include: power miter box (A), circular saw (B) with carbide-tipped blade and Teflon®-coated carbide blade, reciprocating saw (C), ⅜" drill and bits (D), jig saw (E), and screwgun (F). These tools should have heavy-duty motors. Screwgun is designed for driving long deck screws through 2" lumber. Reciprocating saw and power miter box can be purchased at home centers, or leased at tool rental outlets.

Make a map of the features of your house and yard. Include any features that might affect how you build and use your deck, like sun and shade patterns, trees, and other landscaping details. For accurate measurements, use a long tape measure and hold it level and perpendicular to the house.

Creating Site Drawings

Create site drawings of the building area before designing a deck. Show all details that may affect how you build and use the deck.

Building a deck requires two types of site drawings. A **plan view** shows the building site as viewed from directly overhead. An **elevation** shows the vertical details of the site as it is viewed from the side or front.

As you create site drawings, consider how the features of house and yard influence the deck design. Remember that the building site is affected by weather, time of day, and seasonal changes.

For example, if your deck will be used mainly for summertime evening meals, look at the sun, shade, and wind patterns on the site during this time of day.

Everything You Need:

Tools: pencil or marker, eraser, 50-ft. tape measure, ruler, compass, line level.

Materials: large sheets of paper.

Supplies: mason's string.

How to Create Plan-view Site Drawings

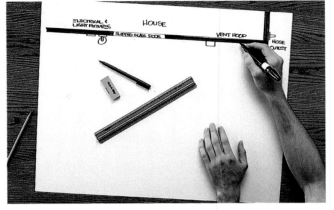

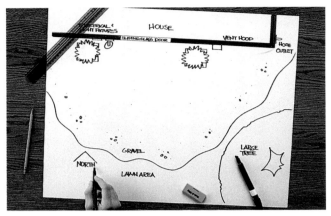

1 Sketch position of house and yard on a large sheet of paper, using a scale of 1" equals 1 foot. Show position of doors, windows, and outdoor utilities, like garden hose spigots, or light fixtures.

2 Add a symbol to the site drawing to indicate north. Mark the location of trees, gardening beds or planters, and any other landscaping features. Show any overhead or underground utility lines.

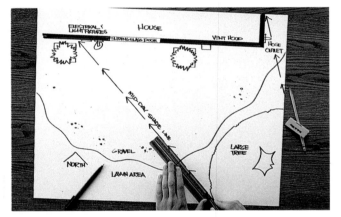

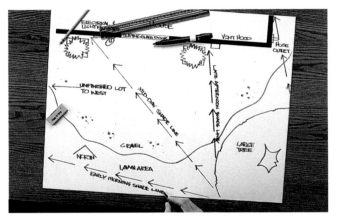

3 Observe the deck site during the time of day when the deck will be used most often. Outline shade and sun patterns on the site drawing.

4 Show how the site changes throughout the day. Outline shade and sun patterns at different times, and quality of nearby view. Note changes in winds, traffic noise, and neighborhood activity.

How to Create Elevation Site Drawings

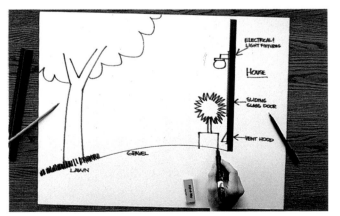

1 Create a side-view elevation map of your site, showing the slope of the ground and the position of the house. For accuracy, stretch level mason's strings from the house, and use the strings for reference to determine slope of ground.

2 Add any other features that will affect how you build and use the deck, like the height of tree branches or telephone wires, shrubs, flowerbeds, or other landscaping details.

23

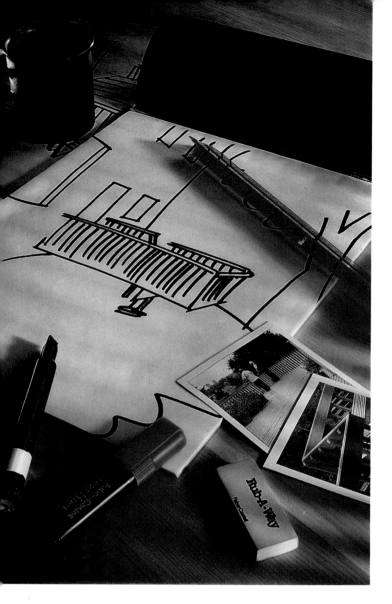

Drawing Design Plans

Design plans help you estimate lumber and hardware needs, and provide the measurements needed to lay out the deck and cut the lumber. If a work permit is required by local codes, you must have design plans.

You will need two types of design drawings for a deck project. A **plan view** shows the parts of the deck as they are viewed from directly overhead. An **elevation** shows the deck parts as viewed from the side or front.

To avoid confusion, do not try to show all parts of the deck in a single plan view. First, draw one plan that shows the outline of the deck and the pattern of the decking boards. Then make another plan that shows the underlying ledger, joists, beams, and posts.

Everything You Need:

Tools: pencil or marker, eraser, ruler.

Materials: site drawing, large sheets of paper, sheets of tissue paper.

How to Draw Design Plans

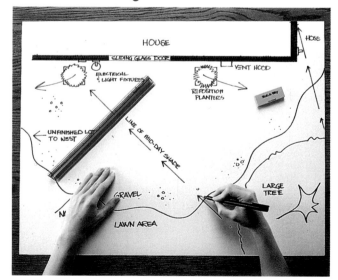

1 Use the scaled site drawings (pages 22 to 23) to help establish the size and shape of the deck.

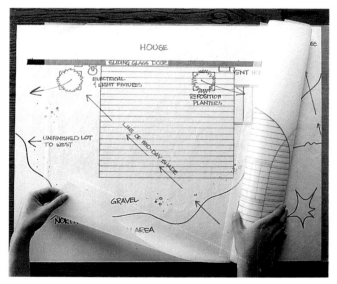

2 Lay a sheet of tissue paper over the site drawing and tape in position. Experiment with deck ideas by sketching different designs on separate sheets of tissue paper.

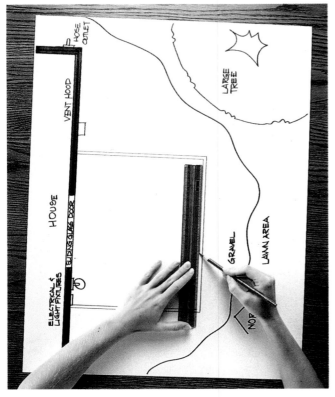

3 Make copies of the scaled site drawing. Use a ruler and sharp pencil to draw the outline of the deck on one copy of the scaled site drawing.

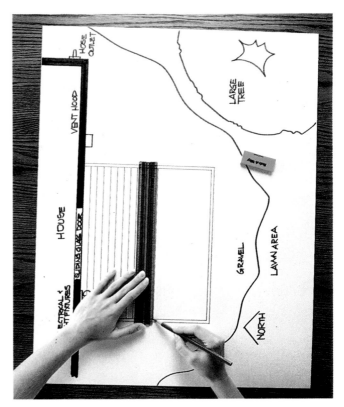

4 Draw in the decking pattern over the outline. Indicate the size and type of lumber and hardware to be used. Save this plan for reference.

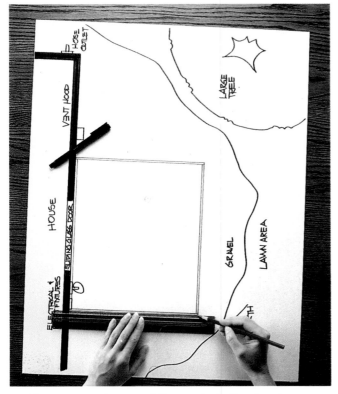

5 On a second copy of the scaled site drawing, draw another outline of the deck. Draw in the ledger, the outside joists, and the header joist.

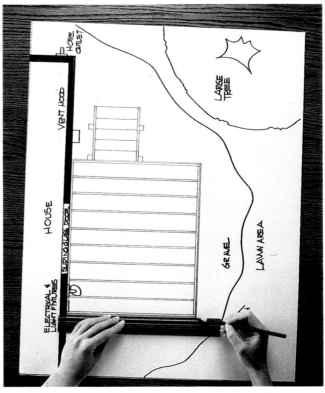

6 Draw the inner joists, and any blocking. Show any facing boards that will be used. Show the stairway stringers, treads, and posts.

(continued next page)

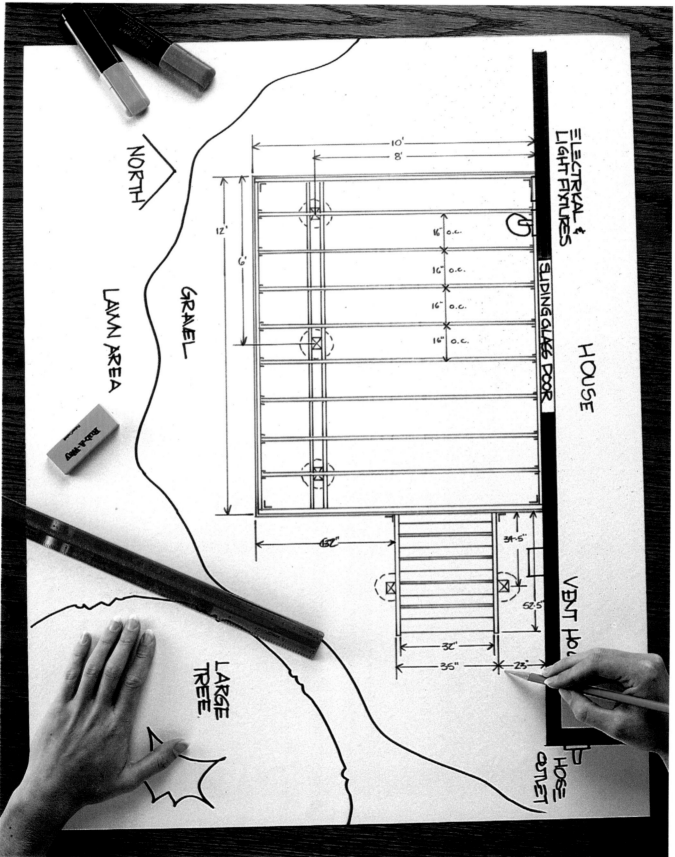

7 Draw in the deck beam and posts, and show the location of the concrete footings. List all deck dimensions on the plan. Save this drawing for reference when ordering lumber and hardware.

26

How to Draw Design Elevations

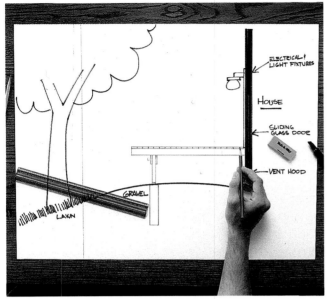

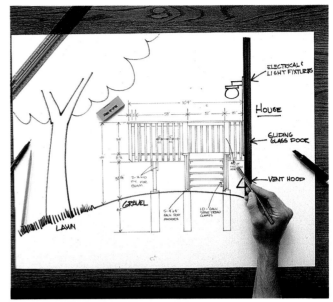

1 Draw in the basic deck platform on the site elevation drawing (page 23). Draw in the beam and the posts.

2 Add the stairway to the elevation drawing, then draw in the railing posts, balusters, rails and caps. List all dimensions on the drawing, and indicate size, type, and quantities of lumber and hardware needed. Save this drawing for reference.

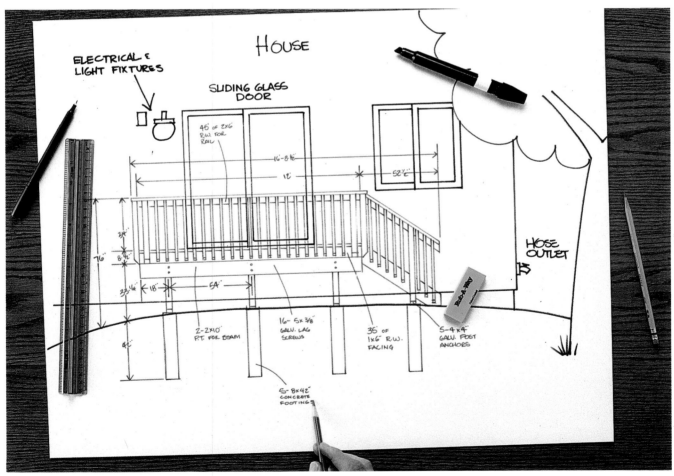

3 Create another design elevation showing the deck as viewed from the front. Include all deck dimensions, and indicate the size and type of lumber and hardware to be used. Save this drawing for reference.

Installing a Ledger

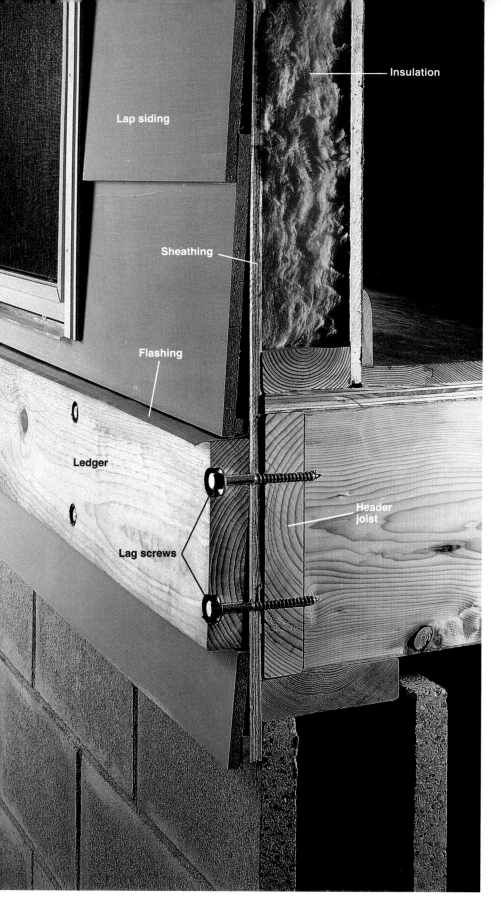

Insulation

Lap siding

Sheathing

Flashing

Ledger

Lag screws

Header joist

NOTE: Before beginnning any project, check with local utilities for the location of underground electrical, telephone, or water lines. Apply for a building permit, where required, and make sure a building inspector has approved the deck design before beginning work.

The first step in building an attached deck is to fasten the ledger to the house. The ledger anchors the deck and establishes a reference point for building the deck square and level. The ledger also supports one end of all the deck joists, so it must be attached securely to the framing members of the house.

Install the ledger so that the surface of the decking boards will be 1" below the indoor floor level. This height difference prevents rainwater or melted snow from seeping into the house.

Everything You Need:

Tools (page 20): pencil, level, circular saw with carbide blade, chisel, hammer, metal snips, caulk gun, drill and bits (¼" twist, 1" spade, ⅜" and ⅝" masonry), ratchet wrench, awl, rubber mallet.

Materials: pressure-treated lumber, galvanized flashing, 8d galvanized common nails, silicone caulk, ⅜" × 4" lag screws and 1" washers, lead masonry anchors for ⅜" lag screws (for brick walls).

Supplies: 2 × 4s for braces.

Ledger (shown in cross section) is made from pressure-treated lumber. Lap siding is cut away to expose sheathing and to provide a flat surface for attaching the ledger. Galvanized flashing tucked under siding prevents moisture damage to wood. Countersunk ⅜" × 4" lag screws hold ledger to header joist inside house.

How to Attach a Ledger to Lap Siding

1 Draw an outline showing where the deck will fit against the house, using a level as a guide. Include the thickness of the outside joists and any decorative facing boards that will be installed.

2 Cut out siding along outline, using a circular saw. Set blade depth to same thickness as siding, so that blade does not cut into sheathing.

3 Use a chisel to finish the cutout where circular saw blade does not reach. Hold the chisel with the bevel-side in.

4 Measure and cut ledger from pressure-treated lumber. Remember that ledger will be shorter than overall length of cutout.

(continued next page)

5 Cut galvanized flashing to length of cutout, using metal snips. Slide flashing up under siding.

6 Center the ledger in the cutout, underneath the flashing. Brace in position, and tack ledger into place with 8d galvanized nails. Apply a thick bead of silicone caulk to crack between siding and flashing.

7 Drill pairs of ¼" pilot holes spaced every 2 feet, through the ledger and sheathing and into the header joist.

8 Counterbore each pilot hole to ½" depth, using a 1" spade bit.

9 Attach ledger to wall with ⅜" × 4" lag screws and washers, using a ratchet wrench.

10 Seal lag screw heads with silicone caulk. Seal the crack between the wall and the sides and bottom of the ledger.

How to Attach a Ledger to Masonry

1 Measure and cut ledger. Ledger will be shorter than overall length of cutout. Drill pairs of ¼" pilot holes every 2 feet in ledger. Counterbore each pilot hole to ½" depth, using a 1" spade bit.

2 Draw an outline of the deck on the wall, using a level as a guide. Center ledger in outline on wall, and brace in position. Mark the pilot hole locations on wall, using an awl or nail. Remove ledger.

(continued next page)

How to Attach a Ledger to Masonry (continued)

3 Drill anchor holes 3" deep into masonry, using a ⅝" masonry bit.

4 Drive lead masonry anchors for ⅜" lag screws into drilled holes, using a rubber mallet.

5 Attach ledger to wall with ⅜" × 4" lag screws and washers, using a ratchet wrench. Tighten screws firmly, but do not overtighten.

6 Seal the cracks between the wall and ledger with silicone caulk. Also seal the lag screw heads.

How to Attach a Ledger to Stucco

1 Draw outline of deck on wall, using a level as a guide. Measure and cut ledger, and drill pilot holes (page 31, step 1). Brace ledger against wall, and mark hole locations, using a nail or awl.

2 Remove ledger. Drill pilot holes through stucco layer of wall, using a ⅜" masonry bit.

3 Extend each pilot hole through the sheathing and into the header joist, using a ¼" bit. Reposition ledger and brace in place.

4 Attach ledger to wall with ⅜" × 4" lag screws and washers, using a ratchet wrench. Seal the lag screw heads and the cracks between the wall and ledger with silicone caulk.

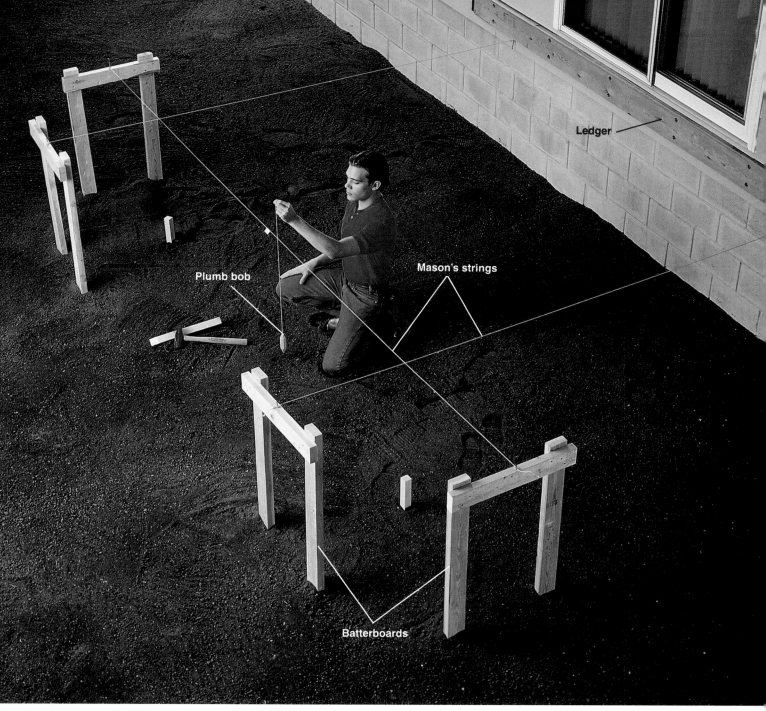

Ledger

Mason's strings

Plumb bob

Batterboards

Mason's strings stretched between ledger and batterboards are used to position footings for deck posts. Use a plumb bob and stakes to mark the ground at the exact centerpoints of footings.

Locating Post Footings

Establish the exact locations of all concrete footings by stretching mason's strings across the site. Use the ledger board as a starting point. These perpendicular layout strings will be used to locate holes for concrete footings, and to position metal post anchors on the finished footings. Anchor the layout strings with temporary 2 × 4 supports, often called batterboards.

Everything You Need:

Tools: tape measure, felt-tipped pen, circular saw, screwgun, framing square, masonry hammer, claw hammer, line level, plumb bob.

Supplies: 2 × 4s, 10d nails, 2½" wallboard screws, mason's strings, masking tape.

How to Locate Post Footings

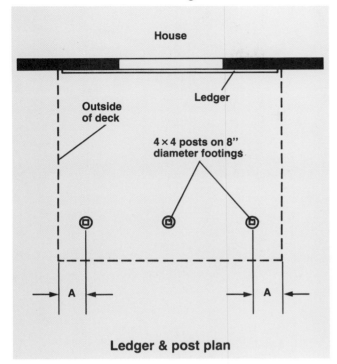

House

Ledger

Outside of deck

4 × 4 posts on 8" diameter footings

A ← | → A

Ledger & post plan

1 Use the design plan (page 26) to find distance (A). Measure from the side of the deck to the center of each outside post. Use the elevation drawings (page 27) to find the height of each deck post.

2 Cut 2 × 4 stakes for batterboards, each about 8" longer than post height. Trim one end of each stake to a point, using a circular saw. Cut 2 × 4 crosspieces, each about 2 feet long.

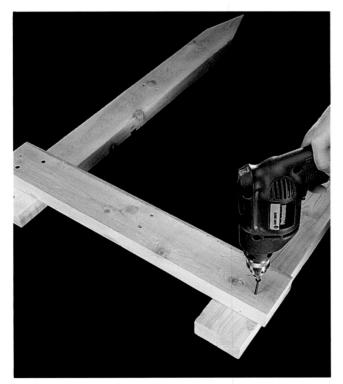

3 Assemble batterboards by attaching crosspieces to stakes with 2½" wallboard screws. Crosspieces should be about 2" below tops of stakes.

4 Transfer measurement A (step 1) to ledger, and mark reference points at each end of ledger. String lines will be stretched from these points on ledger. When measuring, remember to allow for outside joists and facing that will be butted to the ends of the ledger.

(continued next page)

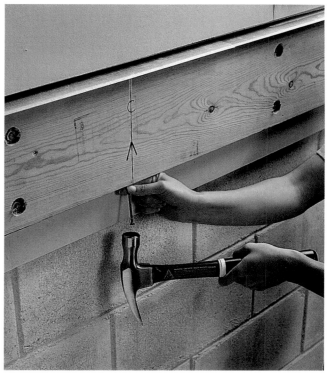

5 Drive a batterboard 6" into the ground, about 2 feet past the post location. Crosspiece of batterboard should be parallel to the ledger.

6 Drive a 10d nail into bottom of ledger at reference point (step 4). Attach a mason's string to nail.

7 Extend the mason's string so that it is taut and perpendicular to the ledger. Use a framing square as a guide. Secure the string temporarily by wrapping it several times around the batterboard.

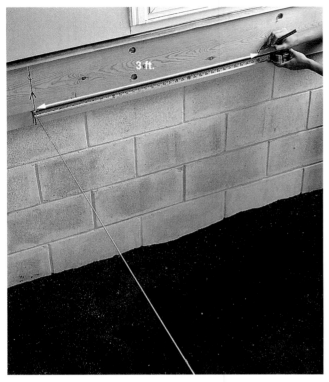

8 Check the mason's string for square using "3-4-5 carpenter's triangle." First, measure along the ledger 3 feet from the mason's string and mark a point, using a felt-tipped pen.

9 Measure mason's string 4 feet from edge of ledger, and mark with masking tape.

10 Measure distance between marks. If string is perpendicular to ledger, the distance will be exactly 5 feet. If necessary, move string left or right on batterboard until distance between marks is 5 feet.

11 Drive a 10d nail into top of batterboard at string location. Leave about 2" of nail exposed. Tie string to nail.

(continued next page)

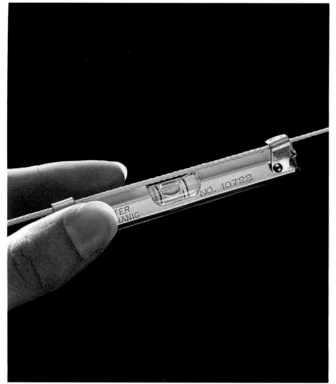

12 Hang a line level on the mason's string. Raise or lower string until it is level. Locate other outside post footing, repeating steps 5 to 12.

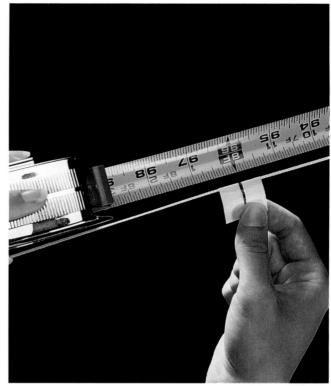

13 Measure along mason's strings from ledger to find centerpoint of posts. Mark centerpoints on strings, using masking tape.

14 Drive additional batterboards into ground, about 2 feet outside mason's strings and lined up with post centerpoint marks (step 13).

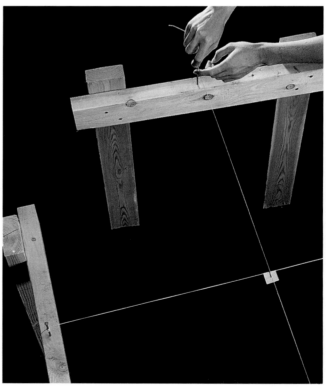

15 Align a third cross string with the centerpoint marks on the first strings. Drive 10d nails in new batterboards, and tie off cross string on nails. Cross string should be close to, but not touching, the first strings.

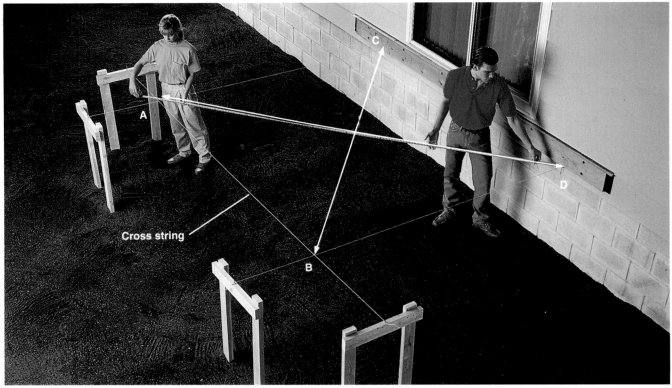

Cross string

16 Check strings for square by measuring distances A-B and C-D. Measure diagonals A-D and B-C from edge of ledger to opposite corners. If strings are square, measurement A-B will be same as C-D, and diagonal A-D will be same as B-C. If necessary, adjust strings on batterboards until square.

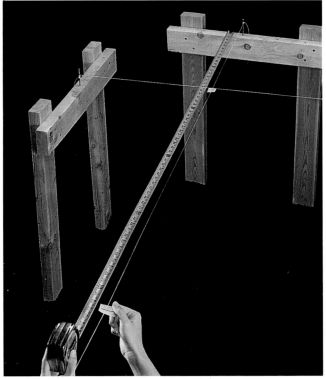

17 Measure along the cross string and mark centerpoints of any posts that will be installed between the outside posts.

18 Use a plumb bob to mark post centerpoints on the ground, directly under the marks on the mason's strings. Drive a stake into ground at each point. Remove mason's strings before digging footings.

Digging & Pouring Footings

Concrete footings hold deck posts in place and support the weight of the deck. Check local codes to determine the size and depth of footings required for your area. In cold climates, footings must be deeper than the soil frost line.

To help protect posts from water damage, each footing should be poured so that it is 2" above ground level. Tube-shaped forms let you extend the footings above ground level.

It is easy and inexpensive to mix your own concrete by combining portland cement, sand, gravel, and water. See pages 18 to 19 for more information on buying and mixing concrete.

Before digging, consult local utilities for location of any underground electrical, telephone, or water lines that might interfere with footings.

Everything You Need:

Tools (page 20): power auger or clamshell posthole digger, tape measure, pruning saw, shovel, reciprocating saw or handsaw, torpedo level, hoe, trowel, shovel, old toothbrush, plumb bob, utility knife.

Materials: 8" concrete tube forms, portland cement, sand, gravel, J-bolts.

Supplies: wheelbarrow, scrap 2 × 4.

Power augers quickly dig holes for post footings. They are available at rental centers. Some models can be operated by one person, while others require two people.

How to Dig & Pour Post Footings

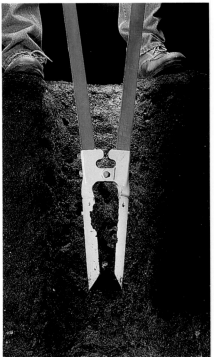

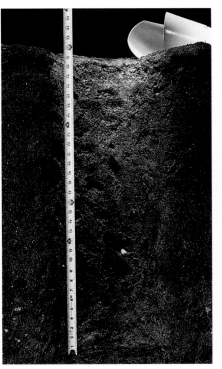

1 Dig holes for post footings with a clamshell digger or power auger, centering the holes on the layout stakes. For holes deeper than 35", use a power auger to dig post-hole footings.

2 Measure hole depth. Local building codes specify depth of footings. Cut away tree roots, if necessary, using a pruning saw.

3 Pour 2" to 3" of loose gravel in the bottom of each footing hole. Gravel will provide drainage under concrete footings.

4 Add 2" to hole depth so that footings will be above ground level. Cut concrete tube forms to length, using a reciprocating saw or handsaw. Make sure cut is straight.

5 Insert tubes into footing holes, leaving about 2" of tube above ground level. Use a level to make sure tops of tubes are level. Pack soil around tubes to hold them in place.

(continued next page)

6 Mix dry ingredients for concrete in a wheelbarrow, using a hoe.

7 Form a hollow in center of dry concrete mixture. Slowly pour a small amount of water into hollow, and blend in dry mixture with a hoe.

8 Add more water gradually, mixing thoroughly until concrete is firm enough to hold its shape when sliced with a trowel.

9 Pour concrete slowly into tube form, guiding concrete from wheelbarrow with a shovel. Use a long stick to tamp the concrete, filling any air gaps in the footing.

10 Level the concrete by pulling a 2 × 4 across the top of the tube form, using a sawing motion. Add concrete to any low spots. Retie the mason's strings on the batterboards, and recheck measurements.

11 Insert a J-bolt at an angle into the wet concrete at center of the footing.

12 Lower the J-bolt slowly into the concrete, wiggling it slightly to eliminate any air gaps.

13 Set the J-bolt so ¾" to 1" is exposed above concrete. Brush away any wet concrete on bolt threads with an old toothbrush.

14 Use a plumb bob to make sure the J-bolt is positioned exactly at center of post location.

15 Use a torpedo level to make sure the J-bolt is plumb. If necessary, adjust the bolt and re-pack concrete. Let concrete cure, then cut away exposed portion of tube with a utility knife.

Setting Posts

Posts support the deck beams and transfer the weight of the deck to the concrete footings. For maximum strength, the posts must be plumb.

To prevent rot or insect damage, use pressure-treated lumber for posts, and make sure the factory-treated end faces down.

Use metal post anchors to attach the posts to the concrete footings. Post anchors have drainage holes and pedestals that raise the ends of the wood posts above the concrete footings.

Everything You Need:

Tools (page 20): pencil, framing square, ratchet wrench, tape measure, power miter box or circular saw, hammer, screwgun, level, combination square.

Materials: metal post anchors, nuts for J-bolts, lumber for posts, 6d galvanized common nails, 2" wallboard screws.

Supplies: long, straight 2 × 4; 1 × 4s; pointed 2 × 2 stakes.

How to Attach Post Anchors

1 Mark the top of each footing as a reference line for installing post anchors. Lay a long, straight 2 × 4 flat across two or three concrete footings, parallel to the ledger, with one edge tight against the J-bolts.

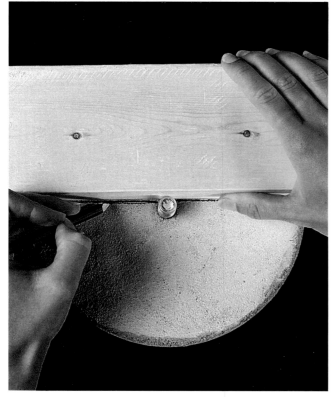

2 Draw a reference line across each concrete footing, using the edge of the 2 × 4 as a guide. Remove the 2 × 4.

3 Place a metal post anchor on each concrete footing, and center it over the J-bolt.

(continued next page)

How to Attach Post Anchors (continued)

4 Use a framing square to make sure the post anchor is positioned square to the reference line drawn on the footing.

5 Thread a nut over each J-bolt, and tighten it securely with a ratchet wrench.

How to Set Posts

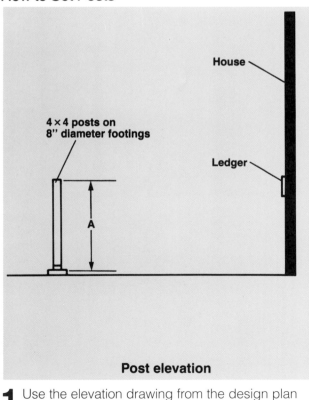

4 × 4 posts on
8" diameter footings

House

Ledger

A

Post elevation

1 Use the elevation drawing from the design plan (page 27) to find the length of each post (A). Add 6" for a cutting margin.

2 Cut posts with power miter box or circular saw. Make sure factory-treated ends of posts are square. If necessary, square them by trimming with a power miter box or circular saw.

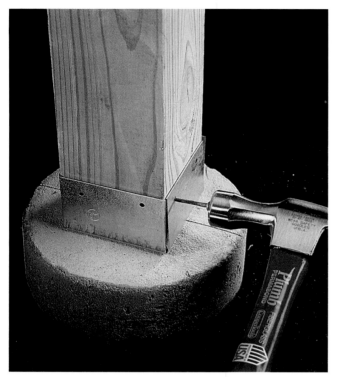

3 Place post in anchor, and tack into place with a single 6d galvanized common nail.

4 Brace post with a 1 × 4. Place the 1 × 4 flat across post, so that it crosses the post at a 45° angle about halfway up.

5 Attach the brace to the post temporarily with a single 2" wallboard screw.

6 Drive a pointed 2 × 2 stake into the ground next to the end of the brace.

(continued next page)

7 Use a level to make sure the post is plumb. Adjust the post, if necessary.

8 Attach the brace to the stake with two 2'' wallboard screws.

9 Plumb and brace the post on the side perpendicular to the first brace.

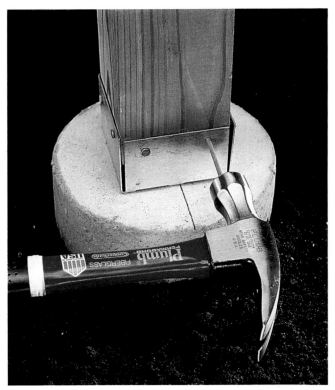

10 Attach the post to the post anchor with 6d galvanized common nails.

11 Position a straight 2 × 4 with one end on ledger and other end across face of post. Level the 2 × 4, then lower its post end ¼" for every 3 ft. between ledger and post (for water runoff). Draw a line on the post along the bottom of the 2 × 4. For cantilevered construction (pages 50 to 52), this line indicates the top of the joists. For corner-post construction (page 53), this line indicates the top of the beam.

12 For cantilevered construction, draw a line as shown in step 11. Then measure down a distance equal to width of joists, and mark the post.

13 Use a square to draw a line completely around the post. This line indicates the top of the cantilever beam.

Installing a Beam

A deck beam is attached to the posts, and helps support the weight of the joists and decking. The method for installing the beam depends on whether the deck is a cantilevered or corner-post design.

A **cantilevered deck** has posts and one or more beams that are set back from the edge of the deck. The advantage is a neater and more attractive appearance. In cantilevered construction, the joists run across and extend past the beam. The general rule is the overhanging, or cantilevered, portion of the deck may be one-third the total length of the joists.

A **corner-post deck** has posts that are set at the edge of the deck. Because joists butt into the beam, rather than run across the top, corner-post construction is ideal for low decks.

Everything You Need:

Tools (page 20): tape measure, pencil, circular saw, paint brush, combination square, screwgun, drill, twist bits (⅛", ¼"), 1" spade bit, ratchet wrench, caulk gun, reciprocating saw or handsaw.

Materials: pressure-treated lumber, clear sealer-preservative, 2½" corrosion-resistant deck screws, ⅜" × 4" lag screws and 1" washers, ⅜" × 5" lag screws (for corner-post deck), silicone caulk.

How to Install a Beam for a Cantilevered Deck

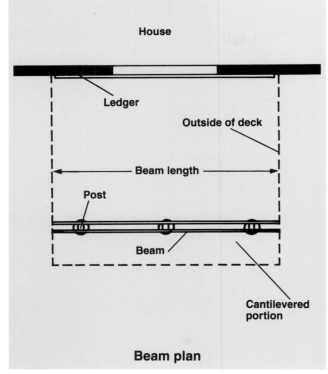

Beam plan

1 Use the deck design plan (page 26) to find the beam length. In plan shown above, the cantilever beam is cut to match overall width of deck.

2 Measure and mark two straight pressure-treated boards to length. Cut boards with a circular saw. Seal cut ends with clear sealer-preservative.

3 Hold beam boards together. Measure and mark the post locations on the tops and sides of boards, using a combination square as a guide.

4 Position one beam board against the sides of the posts with crown side up. Marks on the board should be aligned with beam height marks on posts. Hold board in position with 2½" deck screws.

(continued next page)

5 Drill two ¼" pilot holes through the beam board and into each of the posts.

6 Counterbore each pilot hole to ½" depth, using 1" spade bit.

7 Attach board to posts with ⅜" × 4" lag screws and washers, using a ratchet wrench.

8 Attach the remaining beam board to the opposite sides of the posts, repeating steps 4 to 7. Seal screw heads with silicone caulk.

9 Cut tops of posts flush with top edge of beam, using a reciprocating saw or handsaw. Seal cut ends of posts with clear sealer-preservative.

How to Install a Beam for a Corner-post Deck

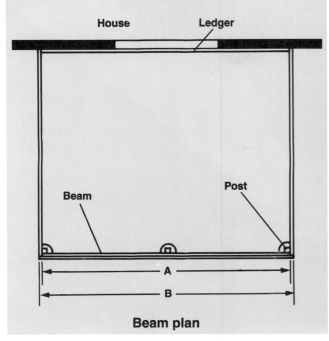

Beam plan

1 Use deck design plan (page 26) to find length of beam. Measure distance (A) between outside edges of corner posts. Mark pressure-treated board to length and cut with circular saw. Cut a second beam board (B), 3" longer than first board. Seal cut ends with clear sealer-preservative.

2 Position shorter beam board against outside of posts so that ends are flush with post edges. Top edge of board should be flush with beam height marks on posts. Drill ⅛" pilot holes, and hold beam board in position with 2½" deck screws.

3 Position the longer beam board against outside of the first board, so that ends overhang by 1½" to allow for outside joists. Fasten boards together with a pair of 2½" deck screws driven every 2 feet.

4 Drill two ¼" pilot holes through both beam boards and into each post. Counterbore each pilot hole to ½" depth, using a 1" spade bit. Secure boards to posts with ⅜" × 5" lag screws and washers, using a ratchet wrench. Seal screw heads and crack between boards with silicone caulk.

Hanging Joists

Joists provide support for the decking boards. In cantilever construction, joists are attached to the ledger and header joist with galvanized metal joist hangers, and are nailed to the top of the beam. In corner-post construction, joists are attached to the ledger and inside of the beam with galvanized joist hangers.

For strength and durability, use pressure-treated lumber for all joists. The exposed outside joists and header joist can be faced with redwood or cedar boards for a more attractive appearance (page 63).

Everything You Need:

Tools (page 20): tape measure, pencil, hammer, combination square, circular saw, paint brush, drill, twist bits (1/16", 1/4"), 1" spade bit.

Materials: pressure-treated lumber, clear sealer-preservative, 10d galvanized common nails, 1¼" joist nails, joist angle brackets, galvanized metal joist hangers, ⅜" × 4" lag screws and 1" washers.

How to Hang Joists

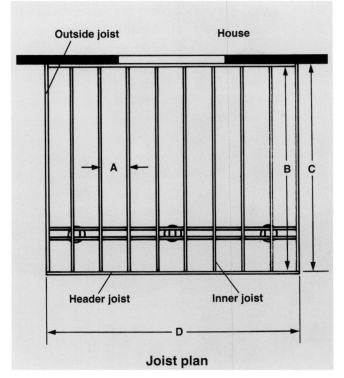

Outside joist   House

A   B   C

Header joist   Inner joist

D

Joist plan

1 Use the design plan (page 26) to find the spacing (A) between joists, and the length of inner joists (B), outside joists (C), and header joist (D). Measure and mark lumber for outside joists, using a combination square as a guide. Cut joists with a circular saw. Seal cut ends with clear sealer-preservative.

2 Drill three ¹⁄₁₆" pilot holes, spaced about 3" apart, through one end of each outside joist.

3 Hold the outside joists in position at ends of ledger with 10d nails driven into the ledger.

4 Attach the outside joists to the top of the beam by toenailing them with 10d nails.

(continued next page)

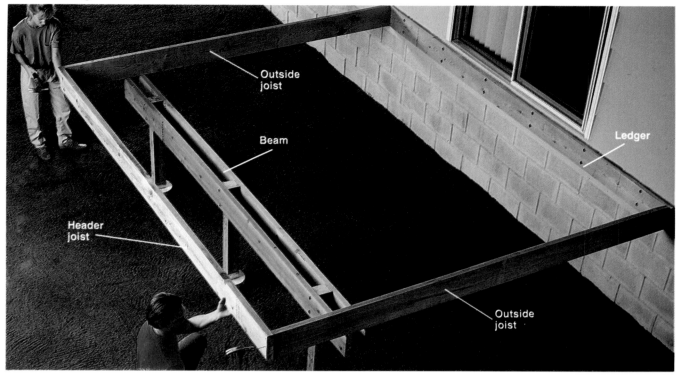

Outside joist

Beam

Ledger

Header joist

Outside joist

5 Measure and cut header joist. Seal cut ends with clear sealer-preservative. Drill 1/16" pilot holes at each end of header joist. Attach header to ends of outside joists with 10d galvanized nails.

6 Strengthen each inside corner of the deck frame with an angle bracket. Attach the brackets with 1¼" joist nails.

Alternate for corner-post deck: Position outside joist against post, flush with end of beam. Drill ¼" pilot holes through end of joist, into post. Counterbore pilot holes to depth of ½"; using 1" spade bit. Attach with ⅜" × 4" lag screws and washers. Cut off posts flush with top of beam, using a reciprocating saw or handsaw.

7 Measure along ledger from edge of outside joist, and mark where joists will be attached to ledger.

8 Draw the outline of each joist on the ledger, using a combination square as a guide.

9 Measure along the beam from outside joist, and mark where joists will cross beam. Draw the outlines across top of both beam boards.

10 Measure along the header joist from the outside joist, and mark where joists will be attached to header joist. Draw the outlines on the inside of the header, using a combination square as a guide.

(continued next page)

11 Attach joist hangers to the ledger and to the header joist. Position each hanger so that one of the flanges is against the joist outline. Nail flange to framing member with 1¼'' joist nails.

12 Cut a scrap board to use as a spacer. Hold spacer inside each joist hanger, then close the hanger around the spacer.

13 Nail the remaining side flange to the framing member with 1¼'' joist nails. Remove spacer.

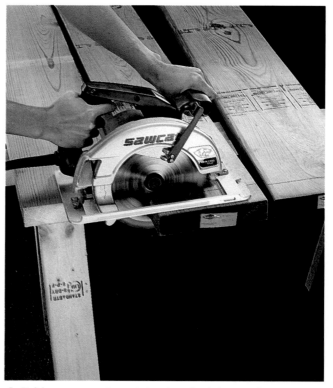

14 Measure and mark lumber for joists, using a combination square as a guide. Cut joists with a circular saw.

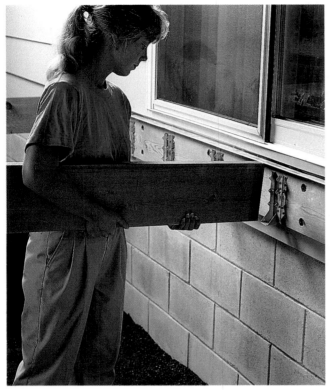

15 Seal cut ends with clear sealer-preservative. Place joists in hangers with crowned side up.

16 Attach the ledger joist hangers to the joists with 1¼'' joist nails. Drive nails into both sides of each joist.

17 Align the joists with the outlines drawn on the top of the beam. Anchor the joists to the beam by toe-nailing from both sides with 10d galvanized nails.

18 Attach the joists to the header joist hangers with 1¼'' joist nails. Drive nails into both sides of each joist.

Laying Decking

How to Lay Decking

Buy decking boards that are long enough to span the width of the deck, if possible. If boards must be butted end-to-end, make sure to stagger the joints so they do not overlap from row to row. Predrill the ends of boards to prevent screws or nails from splitting the wood.

Install decking so there is a ⅛" gap between boards to provide drainage. Boards naturally "cup" as they age (page 11). Lay boards with the bark side facing down, so that the cupped surface cannot hold standing water.

Everything You Need:

Tools (page 20): tape measure, circular saw, screwgun, hammer, drill, ⅛" twist bit, pry bar, chalk line, jig saw or handsaw.

Materials: decking boards, 2½" corrosion-resistant deck screws, galvanized common nails (8d, 10d), redwood or cedar facing boards.

1 Position the first row of decking flush against the house. First decking board should be perfectly straight, and should be precut to proper length. Attach the first decking board by driving a pair of 2½" corrosion-resistant deck screws into each joist.

2 Position remaining decking boards so that ends overhang outside joists. Space boards about ⅛" apart. Attach boards to each joist with a pair of 2½' deck screws driven into each joist.

Alternate method: Attach decking boards with 10d galvanized common nails. Angle the nails toward each other to improve holding power.

(continued next page)

3 If boards are bowed, use a pry bar to lever them into position while fastening.

4 Drill ⅛" pilot holes in ends of boards before attaching them to outside joists. Pilot holes prevent screws from splitting decking boards at ends.

5 After every few rows of decking are installed, measure from edge of the decking board to edge of header joist. If measurements show that the last board will not fit flush against the edge of the deck, adjust board spacing.

6 Adjust board spacing by changing the gaps between boards by a small amount over three or four rows of boards. Very small spacing changes will not be obvious to the eye.

7 Use a chalk line to mark the edge of decking flush with the outside edge of deck. Cut off decking with a circular saw. Set saw blade ⅛" deeper than thickness of decking so that saw will not cut side of deck. At areas where circular saw cannot reach, finish cutoff with a jig saw or handsaw.

8 For a more attractive appearance, face the deck with redwood or cedar facing boards. Miter-cut corners, and attach boards with deck screws or 8d galvanized nails.

Alternate facing technique: Attach facing boards so that edges of decking overhang facing.

Building Stairs

Building deck stairs requires four calculations.

Number of steps depends on the vertical drop of the deck. The vertical drop is the distance from the surface of the deck to the ground.

Rise is the vertical space between treads. Building codes require that the rise measurement be about 7".

Run is the depth of the treads. A convenient way to build deck stairs is to use a pair of 2 × 6s for each tread.

Span is figured by multiplying the run by the number of treads. The span lets you locate the end of the stairway, and position support posts.

Everything You Need:

Tools (page 20): tape measure, pencil, framing square, level, plumb bob, posthole digger, wheelbarrow, hoe, circular saw, hammer, drill, ⅛" twist bit, 1" spade bit, ratchet wrench, caulk gun.

Materials: sand, portland cement, gravel, J-bolts, metal post anchors, 2 × 12 lumber, metal cleats, ¼" × 1¼" lag screws, joist angle brackets, 1¼" galvanized joist nails, ⅜" × 4" lag screws and 1" washers, 2 × 6 lumber, 16d nails, silicone caulk.

Supplies: long, straight 2 × 4; pointed stakes; masking tape.

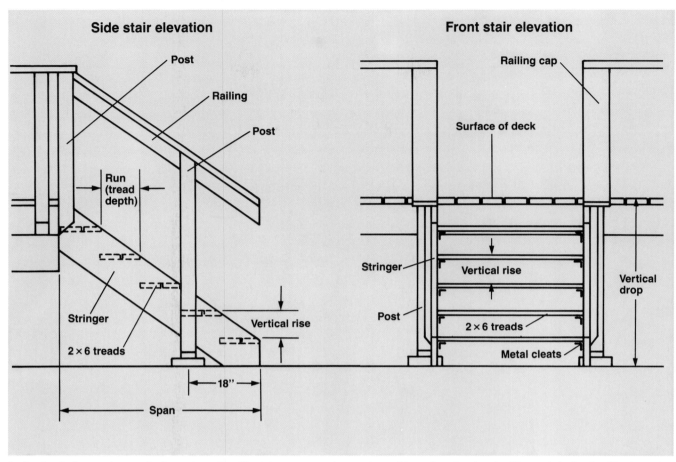

Side stair elevation

Post
Railing
Post
Run (tread depth)
Stringer
2 × 6 treads
Vertical rise
18"
Span

Front stair elevation

Railing cap
Surface of deck
Stringer
Vertical rise
Post
2 × 6 treads
Metal cleats
Vertical drop

A deck stairway is made from two 2 × 12 stringers, and a series of treads attached with metal cleats. Posts set 18" back from the end of the stairway help to anchor the stringers and the railings. Calculations needed to build stairs include the **number of steps**, the **rise** of each step, the **run** of each step, and the stairway **span**.

1. Find the number of steps: Measure vertical drop from deck surface to ground. Divide by 7. Round off to nearest whole number.	Vertical drop:			39"
	÷ 7 =			5.57"
	Number of steps:	=	=	6
2. Find step rise: Divide the vertical drop by the number of steps.	Vertical drop:			39"
	Number of steps:	÷	÷	6
	Rise:	=	=	6.5"
3. Find step run: Typical treads made from two 2 × 6s have a run of 11¼". If your design is different, find run by measuring depth of tread, including any space between boards.	Run:			11¼"
4. Find stairway span: Multiply the run by the number of treads. (Number of treads is always one less than number of steps.)	Run:			11¼"
	Number of treads:	×	×	5
	Span:	=	=	56¼"

How to Build Deck Stairs

1 Use the stairway elevation drawings (page 65) to find measurements for stair stringers and posts. Use a pencil and framing square to outline where stair stringers will be attached to the side of the deck.

2 Locate the post footings so they are 18" back from the end of stairway span. Lay a straight 2 × 4 on the deck so that it is level and square to side of deck. Use a plumb bob to mark the ground at centerpoints of footings.

3 Dig holes and pour footings for posts (pages 40 to 43). Attach metal post anchors to footings and install 4 × 4 posts (pages 44 to 49).

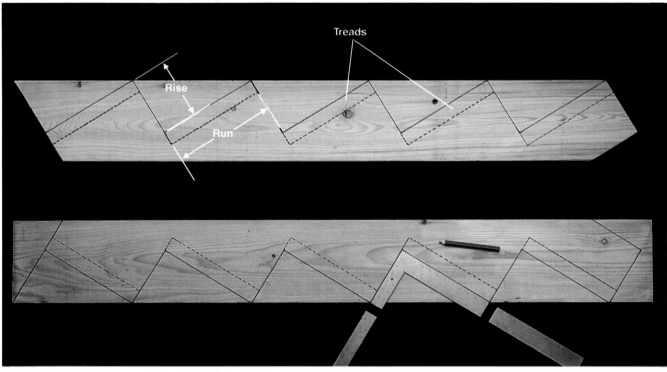

Treads

Rise

Run

4 Lay out stair stringers. Use tape to mark the rise measurement on one leg of a framing square, and the run measurement on the other leg. Beginning at one end of stringer, position the square with tape marks flush to edge of board, and outline the rise and run for each step. Then draw in the tread outline against the bottom of each run line. Use a circular saw to trim ends of stringers as shown.

5 Attach metal tread cleats flush with bottom of each tread outline, using ¼" × 1¼" lag screws. Drill ⅛" pilot holes to prevent the screws from splitting the wood.

6 Attach angle brackets to upper ends of stringers, using 1¼" joist nails. Brackets should be flush with cut ends of stringers.

(continued next page)

7 Position the stair stringers against side of deck, over the stringer outlines. Align top point of stringer flush with the surface of the deck. Attach stringers by nailing the angle brackets to the deck with 1¼" joist nails.

8 Drill two ¼" pilot holes through each stringer and into each adjacent post. Counterbore each hole to depth of ½", using a 1" spade bit. Attach stringers to posts with ⅜" × 4" lag screws and washers, using a ratchet wrench. Seal screw heads with silicone caulk.

9 Measure width of stair treads. Cut two 2 × 6s for each tread, using a circular saw.

10 For each step, position the front 2 × 6 on the tread cleat, so that the front edge is flush with the tread outline on the stringers.

11 Drill ⅛" pilot holes, then attach the front 2 × 6s to the cleats with ¼" × 1¼" lag screws.

12 Position the rear 2 × 6s on the cleats, allowing a small space between boards. Use a 16d nail as a spacing guide. Drill ⅛" pilot holes, and attach 2 × 6s to cleats with ¼" × 1¼" lag screws.

Stair Variations

Hardware option: Metal step brackets can be attached to tops of stringers. This method allows the treads to overhang at the sides.

Notched stringers made of pressure-treated wood are available precut at building centers. Edges of cut-out areas should be coated with sealer-preservative to prevent rot.

Installing a Deck Railing

Railings must be sturdy, and should be firmly attached to the framing members of the deck. Never attach railing posts to the surface decking. Check local building codes for guidelines regarding railing construction. Most codes require that railings be at least 34" above decking. Vertical balusters should be spaced less than 6" apart.

Everything You Need:

Tools (page 20): tape measure, pencil, power miter box, drill, ¼" twist bits (⅛", ¼"), 1" spade bit, combination square, awl, ratchet wrench, caulk gun, level, reciprocating saw or circular saw, jig saw with wood-cutting blade.

Materials: railing lumber (4 × 4s, 2 × 6s, 2 × 4s, 2 × 2s), clear sealer-preservative, ⅜" × 4" lag screws and 1" washers, silicone caulk, 2½" corrosion-resistant deck screws, 10d galvanized common nails.

How to Install a Deck Railing

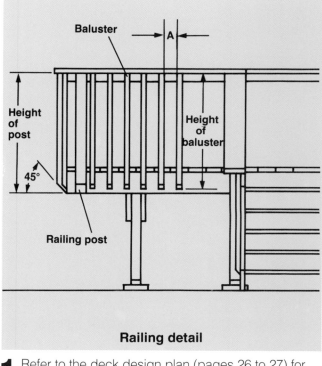

Railing detail

1 Refer to the deck design plan (pages 26 to 27) for spacing (A) and length of railing posts and balusters. Posts should be spaced no more than 6 feet apart.

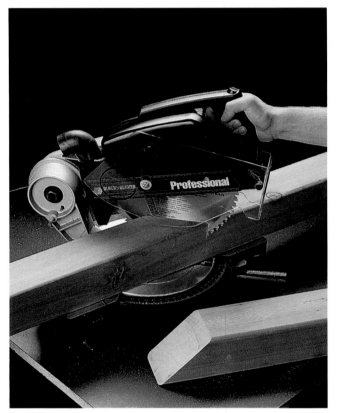

2 Measure and cut 4 × 4 posts, using a power miter box or circular saw. Cut off tops of the posts square, and cut the bottoms at 45° angle. Seal cut ends of lumber with clear sealer-preservative.

3 Measure and cut balusters for main deck, using a power miter box or circular saw. Cut off tops of the balusters square, and cut bottoms at 45° angle. Seal cut ends of lumber with clear sealer-preservative.

4 Drill two ¼" pilot holes through bottom end of each post, spaced 4" apart. Counterbore each pilot hole to ½" depth, using a 1" spade bit.

5 Drill two ⅛" pilot holes near bottom end of each baluster, spaced 4" apart. Drill two ⅛" pilot holes at top of each baluster, spaced 1½" apart.

(continued next page)

6 Measure and mark position of posts around the outside of the deck, using a combination square as a guide. Plan to install a post on outside edge of each stair stringer.

7 Position each post with beveled end flush with bottom of deck. Plumb post with a level. Insert a screwdriver or nail into pilot holes and mark side of deck.

8 Remove post and drill ¼" pilot holes into side of deck.

9 Attach railing posts to side of deck with ⅜" × 4" lag screws and washers, using a ratchet wrench. Seal screw heads with silicone caulk.

10 Measure and cut 2 × 4 side rails. Position rails with edges flush to tops of posts, and attach to posts with 2½" corrosion-resistant deck screws.

11 Join 2 × 4s for long rails by cutting ends at 45° angle. Drill ¹⁄₁₆" pilot holes to prevent nails from splitting end grain, and attach rails with 10d galvanized nails. (Screws may split mitered ends.)

12 Attach ends of rails to stairway posts, flush with edges of posts, as shown. Drill ⅛" pilot holes, and attach rails with 2½" deck screws.

13 At stairway, measure from surface of decking to the top of the upper stairway post (A).

14 Transfer measurement A to lower stairway post, measuring from the edge of the stair stringer.

(continued next page)

15 Position 2 × 4 rail against inside of stairway posts. Align rail with top rear corner of top post, and with the pencil mark on the lower post. Have a helper attach rail temporarily with 2½" deck screws.

16 Mark the outline of the post and the deck rail on the back side of the stairway rail.

17 Mark the outline of the stairway rail on the lower stairway post.

18 Use a level to mark a plumb cutoff line at the bottom end of the stairway rail. Remove the rail.

19 Extend the pencil lines across both sides of the stairway post, using a combination square as a guide.

20 Cut off lower stairway post along diagonal cutoff line, using a reciprocating saw or circular saw.

21 Use a jig saw to cut the stairway rail along the marked outlines.

22 Position the stairway rail flush against top edge of posts. Drill ⅛" pilot holes, then attach rail to posts with 2½" deck screws.

(continued next page)

23 Use a spacer block to ensure equal spacing between balusters. Beginning next to a plumb railing post, position each baluster tight against spacer block, with top of baluster flush to top of rail. Attach each baluster with 2½" deck screws.

24 For stairway, position baluster against stringer and rail, and adjust for plumb. Draw diagonal cutoff line on top of baluster, using top of stair rail as a guide. Cut baluster on marked line, using power miter box. Seal ends with clear sealer-preservative.

25 Beginning next to upper stairway post, position each baluster tight against spacer block, with top flush to top of stair rail. Attach baluster with 2½" deck screws.

26 Position 2 × 6 cap so edge is flush with inside edge of rail. Drill ⅛" pilot holes, and attach cap to rail with 2½" deck screws driven every 12". Also drive screws into each post and into every third baluster. For long caps, bevel ends at 45°. Drill 1/16" pilot holes, and attach at post using 10d nails.

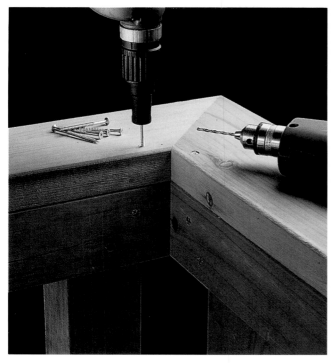

27 At corners, miter ends of railing cap at 45°. Drill ⅛" pilot holes, and attach cap to post with 2½" deck screws.

28 At top of stairs, cut cap so that it is flush with stairway rail. Drill ⅛" pilot holes and attach cap with 2½" deck screws.

29 Measure and cut cap for stairway rail. Mark outline of post on side of cap, and bevel-cut the ends of the cap.

30 Position cap over the stairway rail and balusters so that edge of cap is flush with inside edge of rail. Drill ⅛" pilot holes, and attach cap to rail with 2½" deck screws driven every 12". Also drive screws through cap into stair post and into every third baluster.

Lumber & Materials Checklist

Item	Size, type	Quantity	Where to buy	Price each	Total price
Lumber					
Ledger					
Posts					
Beams					
Joists					
Decking					
Stair stringers					
Stair treads					
Railing posts					
Balusters or rails					
Hardware					
Flashing					
Galvanized nails					
1¼" joist nails					
Post anchors					
Lag screws					
Deck screws					
Joist hangers					
Joist angle brackets					
Metal stair cleats					
Concrete					
Concrete forms					
Portland cement					
Sand					
Gravel					
Miscellaneous					
Silicone caulk					
Sealer/stain					
Equipment rental					
Tools to buy					

Photocopy this checklist for reference when ordering lumber and materials.

Index

A

Anchors,
  masonry, 17
  post, 17
Angle brackets, 17
  building stairs, 64, 67-68
  hanging joists, 54, 56
Angled joist hangers, 17
Awl, 20

B

Balusters, 4-5, 9, 70-71
Batterboards, 34-39
Beams, 4
  installation, 50-53
  plan for cantilever construction, 51
  plan for corner-post construction, 53
  size, 15
  span, 15
Blocking, 6-7
Border decking pattern, 7
Boxed steps, 8
Brackets, angle, 17
Building codes, 4, 8-9, 40, 70
Building decks, 28-77
Building supplies, 78

C

Cantilevered deck,
  beam installation, 50-52
  beam plan, 51
  hanging joists, 54-59
  setting posts, 44-49
Cap, railing, 4-5, 9
  size, 15
Carpenter's triangle, 37
Cat's paw, 20
Caulk gun, 20
Caulking,
  beam installation, 50, 52
  building stairs, 64, 68
  ledger installation, 28, 30-33
  railing installation, 72
CCA (chromated copper arsenate),
  10, 12
Cedar, 4, 10, 12-13
  facing boards, 63
  joists, 54
Chalk line, 20, 61, 63
Chisel, 20
  ledger installation, 28-29
Circular saw, 21
Clamshell posthole digger, 20
  building stairs, 64
  digging footings, 40-41

Claw hammer, 20, 34, 36
Cleats, 4, 8, 17, 64-65, 67, 69
Combination square, 20
  beam installation, 50-5⁻
  hanging joists, 54-55, 57
  railing installation, 72, 75
  setting posts, 44, 49
Compass, 20
Concrete, 18-19
  footings, 4, 40, 42-43, 64, 66
  tube forms, 40-43
Corner-post deck,
  beam installation, 50, 53
  beam plan, 53
  hanging joists, 54-59
  setting posts, 46-49

D

Deck basics, 4-21
Deck design, 24-27
Deck fasteners, 16
Deck parts, 4-5
Deck planning, 14-15, 22-27
Decking, 4-5
  boards, 15, 61
  facing, 63
  laying, 61-63
  patterns, 6-7
  span, 15
Design and planning, 22-27
Design plan, 24-27
  beam installation, 51, 53
  joists, 55
  railing installation, 70
Diagonal decking pattern, 6
Diamond-pattern deck, 6
Digging footings, 40-43
Double joists, 6-7
Drill, 21

E

Elevation drawings,
  design, 22, 24, 27, 46
  post, 46
  site, 52-53
  stairway, 65
End grain, decking boards, 11
Eye protection, 12, 21

F

Facing boards, 4-5, 61, 63
Fasteners, 16-17
Flashing, 17, 28, 30
Flat pry bar, 20
Footings, 4
  attaching post anchors, 44-46
  buying and mixing concrete,
    18-19
  digging and pouring, 40-43

  locating, 34-39, 66
Framed opening, decking, 7
Framing square, 20

G

Galvanized hardware, 16-17
Grade stamp, 12-13

H

Hammers, 20
  masonry, 34, 36, 38
Handrails, 9
Hardware, 16-17
Header joists, 4
  hanging, 55-56
  ledger installation, 28, 30, 33
Heartwood, 10, 13
Hoe, 20
Hydraulic jack, 21

I

Installing a beam, 50-53
Installing a deck railing, 70-77
Installing the ledger, 28-33

J

J-bolts, 16-17
  building stairs, 64
  pouring footings, 40, 43
Jig saw, 21
Joist hangers, 5, 16-17
  hanging joists, 54, 58-59
Joists, 4-5
  decking patterns, 6-7
  double, 6-7
  hanging, 72-77
  header, 4, 28, 30, 33, 56
  outside, 4-5, 56
  plan, 55
  short, 7
  size and spacing, 15, 55
  span, 15
  trim, 7

K

Knots, lumber, 10-11

L

Lag screws, 16-17
Landings, 8
Lap siding, ledger installation,
  28-31
Lattice panels, 9
Laying decking, 61-63
Ledger plan, 35
Ledgers, 4-5

installation, 28-33
Levels, 20, 22
Line level, 20, 22, 34, 38
Locating post footings, 34-39
Lumber,
  basics, 10-11
  cedar, 4, 10-13, 54, 61, 63
  end grain, 11
  flaws, 11
  heartwood, 10, 13
  ordering, 78
  preservatives, 10-13
  pressure-treated, 4, 10-13, 44, 50, 54
  redwood, 4, 10, 12-13, 54, 61, 63
  sapwood, 10, 13
  size, 14-15
  span, 15
  storage, 11
  types, 12-13
Lumber and materials checklist, 78

M
Masonry, ledger installation, 31-32
Masonry anchors, 17, 32
Mason's string, 20
  post footings location, 34, 36-39
  site drawings, 22-23
Materials, ordering, 78
Metal snips, 20

N
Nails, 16

O
Open steps, 8
Orbital sander, 21
Ordering lumber and materials, 78
Outside joists, 4-5, 56

P
Parquet decking pattern, 6
Particle mask, 12, 21
Plan-view drawings, 22-26
Platform steps, 8
Plumb bob, 20
  building stairs, 64, 66
  post footings location, 34, 39
  pouring footings, 40, 43
Portland cement, 18-19, 40-43
Post anchors, 4-5, 16-17
  attaching posts, 47-48
  building stairs, 64, 66
  installation, 44-46
Post elevation plan, 46
Post footings, 4
  concrete, 18-19
  digging and pouring, 40-43

location, 34-39, 66
Post plan, 35
Posts, 4-5
  railings, 9
  setting, 44, 46-49
  size, 14-15
Pouring footings, 40-43
Power augers, digging footings, 40-41
Power drill, 21
Power miter box, 21
Premixed concrete, 18-19
Preshaped products, 9
Pressure sprayer, 21
Pressure-treated lumber, 10-12
  beams, 4, 50-51
  joists, 4, 54
  ledgers, 4, 28-29
  posts, 4, 44
Pruning saw, 40-41
Pry bar, 20, 61-62
Putty knife, 20

R
Railing posts, 4-5, 9
  size and spacing, 15
Railings, 4-5, 9
  horizontal, 9
  installation, 70-77
  plan, 70
  preshaped, 9
  size, 15
Ratchet wrench, 20
Ready-mixed concrete, 18-19
Reciprocating saw, 21
Redwood, 4, 10, 12-13
  facing boards, 61, 63
  header joists, 54
Rise, stairs, 64-65
Rubber mallet, 20, 28, 32
Run, stairs, 64-65

S
Sander, orbital, 21
Sapwood, 10, 13
  sealer-preservative, 10, 13
Saws, 21
Scratch awl, 20
Screwgun, 21
Screws, 16
Sealer-preservative, 10-11, 13
Sheathing, ledger installation, 28, 30, 33
Silicone caulk, 16-17
Site drawings, 22-23
Span, stairs, 15, 64-65
Span limits, 14-15
Stair cleats, 17
Stairs, building, 64-69
  span, 64-65

Stairways, 4-5, 8
  measurements, 65
Steps, 8
  boxed, 8
  brackets, 67, 69
  number of, 64-65
  open, 8
  platform, 8
Stringers, 4-5, 8, 65
  notched, 8, 69
  size, 15
Stucco, ledger installation, 33

T
Tools,
  basics, 21
  beam installation, 50
  building stairs, 64
  design drawings, 24
  digging and pouring footings, 40
  hand, 20-21
  hanging joists, 54
  laying decking, 61
  ledger installation, 28
  post anchor attachment, 44
  post footings location, 34
  power, 21
  railing installation, 70
  setting posts, 44
  site drawings, 22
Torpedo level, 20, 43, 74
Treads, 4-5, 8, 64-65, 68-69
Trim joists, 7
Trowel, 20

U
Utility lines, 40

V
Vacuum, 21
Vertical drop, stairs, 64-65
Vertical rise, 64-65

W
Washers, 16

Cowles Creative Publishing, Inc.
offers a variety of how-to books.
For information write:
  Cowles Creative Publishing
  Subscriber Books
  5900 Green Oak Drive
  Minnetonka, MN 55343